Faith on the Edge Series

The Quest
for Spirituality

Adam Francisco

CONCORDIA PUBLISHING HOUSE • SAINT LOUIS

Written by Adam Francisco

Edited by Edward Engelbrecht

3 4 5 6 7 8 9 10   11 10 09 08 07 06

CONTENTS

About This Series

In the past, science served as a stepchild of alchemy, a handmaiden of theology, and a tool of industry. At the beginning of the twentieth century, science took on a new role. Science became the answer to all humankind's problems. The priests and priestesses of science pulled on their white lab coats, prophesied through their theories, and consecrated each new discovery or invention. Humans marveled.

In response to these new inventions, a new type of literature arose—science fiction, which sometimes warned us about the maddening pace of technology. The robot would replace the human worker. Nuclear fallout would devastate life on earth. Science would solve people's problems by doing away with people, or at least by doing away with their humanity.

Today, people remain thankful for science. But they also recognize that science does not hold all the answers. In fact, they see that science can raise more questions than it answers, driving people on further quests for understanding, truth, and contentment.

The Faith on the Edge Bible study series tracks the progress of science and people's fascinations and fears about science. Each session introduces a contemporary topic, summarizes what science has to say about it, and then provides biblical answers and guidance so that you can face the future with the wisdom and confidence that only God can provide.

Student Introduction

Jai guru deva.
—the Maharishi

Four days in August 1967 made eastern spirituality a permanent part of western subculture. The Maharishi Mahash Yogi announced that he would give a final lecture on transcendental meditation before he took a vow of silence. The Beatles rock group rushed to catch the lecture. The next day, they followed the Maharishi on retreat in Wales to learn his technique for meditation. While they were on retreat, the Beatles' friend and manager, Brian Epstein, suddenly died. And the icons of British rock and roll publicly committed themselves to the quest for enlightenment.

Since the cultural ferment of the late 1960s, new types of spirituality have spiced western religious life like saffron-topped burgers or curry-filled hot dogs. Today's quest for spirituality is sophisticated, combining science-based methods and ancient traditions to offer more credible approaches.

This study will introduce you to several of the most popular quests for spirituality. It will critique their claims and consider them in view of the teachings of the Bible. It will reveal to you God's quest, how in loving kindness He seeks you through His Son, Jesus Christ.

Oh, and incidentally, the Maharishi never took that vow of silence in the summer of 1967.

The editor

Spiritual Encounters

In the Book of Acts, St. Luke records early Christian encounters with unbelief. In one episode, the apostle Paul visited the center of Greek culture—Athens. While Paul waited for his traveling companions, he noticed the Athenians' fervent spirituality (Acts 17:16–34). In response, Paul "reasoned in the synagogue with the Jews and the God-fearing Greeks, as well as in the marketplace day by day with those who happened to be there" (17:17).

When faced with objections from Jewish people, Paul argued from the Old Testament to demonstrate that Jesus was in fact the promised Messiah. When faced with other brands of spirituality, Paul took a different approach. Before the people and philosophers of Athens, Paul used man's natural knowledge of God to teach the Athenians about their spiritual needs. He quoted pagan philosophers and poets to connect with his audience. Only then did he point to Jesus Christ as the answer for full and certain knowledge of God.

The spiritual fervor of today is not unlike the religious fervor of ancient Athens. New or renewed religious beliefs appear each day. False religions and superstition threaten the unwary. Contemporary spirituality offers answers to spiritual questions and even claims scientific backing.

However, spirituality not established by the Creator lacks a firm foundation. True spirituality is grounded in and shaped by Christ. How do Christians testify to this spirituality? The apostle Peter writes, "In your hearts set apart Christ as Lord. Always be prepared to give an answer to everyone who asks you to give the reason for the hope that you have" (1 Peter 3:15). Peter exhorts Christians to always be ready to defend Christian hope. The famous church reformer Martin Luther wrote, "Therefore it follows from this that every Christian should account for his faith and be able to give a reason and an answer when necessary" (*Luther's Works* 30:105).

Ready to Speak

In an age of increasing spirituality, the Christian faith stands ready to give solid answers about God and His relationship to humanity. God's appearing in the flesh through Jesus Christ takes away the need for spiritual speculation. Jesus assures us of our standing before God and the genuine spirituality that follows. When circumstances call upon us to testify to this truth, we must be ready.

Readiness takes training. Luther wrote that when you "have to engage in controversy . . . you must use all your cleverness and effort and be as profound and subtle a controversialist as possible" (LW 26:30–31). As you journey into the world of contemporary spirituality, you will encounter many spiritual claims. Familiarity with spiritual trends and the ability to critique them are necessary skills. Perhaps the most basic skill you will need is the ability to apply God's Law and God's solution in the Gospel.

Apart from Jesus, the human quest for spirituality is doomed to failure. However, a prepared Christian can act as a guide for someone lost on the journey.

Adam Francisco

Enlightened

T hey hold hands. Incense billows about the room. Sitting silently in a circle, the three radio hosts prepare for the Saturday night broadcast of *ShadoWorlds: Chronicles of the Paranormal.*

Once the hosts reach a state of enlightenment, they are ready to begin their three-hour discussion on spirituality. Occasionally, Wiccan priestesses, tarot card readers, numerologists, dream interpreters, and other guests join the show. Listeners phone in and participate. The goal: to attain spiritual enlightenment through paranormal experiences.

Ideas expressed on *ShadoWorlds* illustrate a steadily growing spiritual worldview. In matters where traditional religion remains silent, enlightened spirituality whispers answers. It offers explanations about the unknown.

The mysteries of the paranormal are said to expand our spiritual horizons. For example, Extrasensory Perception (ESP) enables a person to contact spirit guides in order to map past lives. Mediums contact deceased loved ones to ease the grieving process. Mental telepathy and telekinesis result from parapsychological abilities. Astrologers, tarot card readers, numerologists, dream interpreters, and others provide insight into future events. Aura readers and psychic surgeons heal the body, and hypnotism heals the mind.

1. In your social and professional circle, how popular is this form of spirituality? What do you think accounts for its popularity?

2. How do you think *ShadoWorlds* listeners and those who seek this type of enlightened spirituality think about life? In other words, how do they view life and the world around them?

Enlightened spirituality has a *monistic* worldview. Monism affirms a oneness to reality. That is, all things share the same essence. Everything that exists, according to monism, exists eternally.

Monists believe humans can connect to all things past, present, and future. Drawing from universal psychic energy, modern spiritualists claim that they can contact eternally existing spirit beings. For example, a person's fate can be known by reading tarot cards. Dreams can offer insight into past and future events. If people are enlightened enough, they are able to connect to hidden sources of knowledge that lie somewhere within the whole of reality.

A recent *U.S. News and World Report* article states that religion and spirituality in America are "as important as ever, no matter what you believe."

3. Take some time to discuss this quote. What are its implications for the current study? What are its implications for classic Christian spirituality?

The article includes charts and graphs from the *Britannica Book of the Year 2001* that show how Americans think about religious and spiritual matters. Individuals are asked questions about the truth of one's particular religion, how often one feels God's presence or a spiritual force, and so on. One person interviewed in the article states that disbelief does not characterize Americans. He says that Americans will believe anything. A chart tracking the growth of non-Christian religions proudly notes: "The more the merrier."

A Light on the Hidden and Uncertain

Today's enlightened spirituality recognizes the ability of people to experience the *paranormal*. According to this view, profound spiritual insight lies in the realm of the unknown. People emerge from these encounters awakened to their true self and the true nature of reality.

Beginning in the nineteenth century, scientists and psychologists have studied unexplainable, extraordinary events. Early on, psychologist and philosopher William James amassed evidence about the reality of paranormal experience. In the late 1920s, Clark University in Massachusetts held a symposium on paranormal events. Included in the panel of presenters, and an avid supporter of paranormal research, was Sir Arthur Conan Doyle, author of the Sherlock Holmes stories. With the exception of two presenters, all the experts were convinced of at least the possibility, if not the certainty, of genuine paranormal experiences.

The 1960s saw tremendous growth in paranormal research. Universities such as Stanford and Duke led the way and still continue to engage in rigorous scientific tests of paranormal experiences. Many scientific studies on the paranormal lend credibility to its acceptance. However, careful analysis raises important questions about these studies.

Though scientific research has established some credibility for paranormal events, psychologists raise doubts about their regularity. *The Journal of Research for Psi Phenomena* published an essay in 1979 that revealed difficulties in distinguishing these experiences. The author, M. A. Persinger, noted that paranormal experiences are usually accompanied by excessive emotional reactions. Persinger suggested that these traumatic and emotion-laden experiences weaken critical thinking skills. This causes people to offer a paranormal interpretation for an otherwise normal event. In other words, the event was "normal," but the person's thought about the event was "paranormal."

Lawyer and theologian John W. Montgomery brings to light certain philosophical and historical problems with paranormal experiences. In his book *Principalities and Powers* he argues that the term *paranormal* is now used to describe events that were once attributed to supernatural forces (angels, demons, or God). He attributes this to an anti-supernatural bias.

Though some unexplained events are best attributed to paranormal phenomena, Montgomery raises the question: how do we know that paranormal experiences are not encounters with demonic supernatural forces? Establishing a supernatural cause for events is outside the sphere of scientific proof. Montgomery's analysis shows the difficulty of establishing differences between paranormal and supernatural events.

Paranormal events are, by definition, unexplainable. Causes and explanations for the paranormal remain concealed. The Latin word that means "concealed," *occultus*, gives us our word *occult*. Enlightened spirituality parallels and commingles with the world of the occult. Like the Ouija boards found in children's toy stores, paranormal experience may appear harmless and even scientific. However, you never know what spiritual force lurks in the unknown.

To be sure, the Holy Scriptures and the Christian faith affirm an invisible reality. For example, the ancient Nicene Creed confessed that within God's creation there exists things visible and invisible, seen and unseen. The Scriptures record angelic appearances and angelic discussions with humans. Christians do not deny an "invisible" element to creation. Yet the unseen typically remains "unseen" in Christian thought.

4. Compare and contrast the *ShadoWorlds* method and knowledge of perceiving the unseen with the Christian method.

When criticized, those who claim knowledge of paranormal events insist that a person must achieve enlightenment in order to experience and correctly perceive and interpret the paranormal. In other words, you've got to try it to know it is real.

5. What are some dangers in trying spiritual options in order to prove they are true? Does Christianity ask the same thing of a person, that is, "Try it and you'll know it is true"?

The Darkness of Uncertainty

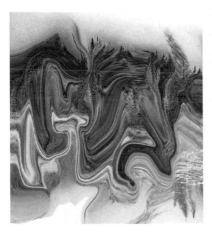

Modern paranormal spirituality appeals to many people. It proposes answers where traditional religion and science are silent. Such spirituality appeals to many Christians as well. Contemporary spiritualists use Christian terminology, pray, and read Scripture. Yet the worldview of contemporary spirituality, even though it uses Christian terms, opposes the worldview of classic Christian spirituality.

Contemporary enlightened spirituality finds God's revelation insufficient. Unsatisfied with a humble trust in God, modern spiritualists turn away from faith in the Creator and trust answers they arrive at through their spiritual quest.

Consider the following story. A starved man is placed in a pitch-black room. He is told that there is food and a black cat in the room. He feels something rub against his leg. He concludes that this must be the black cat. He reaches down to pet the cat and learns that the cat is much larger than he expected. In fact, the cat is a panther, and the man is the food!

Modern spirituality encourages people to enter the room of the paranormal to find spiritual sustenance. But the paranormal remains unexplained and uncertain. It keeps people in the dark and in spiritual danger. Their trust turns from God's certain Word to hidden and uncertain realities.

6. Read Jesus' parable of the wise and foolish builders in Matthew 7:24–27. Compare the uncertainty of contemporary spirituality with the actions of the builders. Reflect on how Christian spirituality builds on certainty.

7. What are the short-term results of building without a foundation? What are the eternal consequences for a person's soul?

Faith built on uncertain and wavering spiritual experiences and the endeavors of humans is doomed to destruction. Without certainty, there is no light. Without light, there is no hope.

8. What are some examples where an enlightened spirituality appears to be compatible with the Christian faith? Have you ever found it appealing? Give examples.

9. Spiritual realities remain hidden from our eyes. How can we be sure they exist? Who alone can be the ultimate authority on spirituality?

10. The Book of Proverbs says, "Wisdom is supreme; therefore get wisdom. Though it cost all you have, get understanding" (Proverbs 4:7). How and where do we get spiritual wisdom and understanding?

Shedding Light on the Darkness

C laims of extraordinary events grab our attention. New scientific discoveries or paranormal events challenge our views of nature and reality. However, much remains in the dark.

The darkness of the human situation prods us to seek God (Acts 17:27). Questions about human identity and future events motivate our quest for spirituality. Throughout the history of humankind, God has graciously delayed His rightful judgment of our ignorance and disobedience. Finally, in one decisive event, He called all people from spiritual darkness into "His wonderful light" (1 Peter 2:9).

In Jesus Christ, God Himself is manifested. Jesus illuminates the hiddenness of God. All that we need to know concerning humanity and spirituality comes to light in Jesus. "This is the verdict: Light has come into the world. . . . Whoever lives by the light comes into the light, so that it may be seen plainly that what he has done has been done through God" (John 3:19, 21). The focal point of this light shines on the cross at Calvary.

On the cross we see God as He identifies with the human situation. He came to us as a man. He suffered as man suffers. He faced death as man faces imminent death. He died as man dies. And He returned to the dust as man returns to the dust. If this were the end of the story, our situation would remain the same. The search for authentic and enlightened spirituality would continue in the darkness of doubt and uncertainty. However, something extraordinary and unexplainable happened. The disciples saw Jesus three days after His death on the cross. He rose from the dead!

This changed everything. Jesus' claim to be equivalent with God the Father had new meaning. His claim to *be* the only true spirituality meant something different (John 14:6). The Scriptures had new meaning. Our situation had new meaning.

The consequences of sin, namely death, were overturned. Jesus' death and resurrection assure us of a right standing before God for all eternity. True spirituality radiates from His cross. Our spirituality has a visible starting and ending point in Christ on the cross.

11. Christian spirituality is certified in Jesus' resurrection. Read John 2:22. What are the disciples assured of after Jesus' resurrection?

The truth of the Christian faith depends on Christ's resurrection from the dead (1 Corinthians 15:14, 17). The Christian faith is, in principle, falsifiable. What does this mean? You can check the truthfulness of the Gospel with actual historic events. Instead of guessing what God is like and what He is capable of doing, Christians can speak positively of God because of the things He has done in history.

Other religions make claims about God and human spirituality, but they remain empty assertions because there are no witnesses. For example, Muhammed claimed to have received revelations from God. These words were recorded in the Qur'an. The Mormon Joseph Smith claimed to have found golden tablets, which recorded a visit by Jesus to early America. Gautama, the Buddha, claimed that nirvana is achieved through Dharma. A host of other spiritual and religious claims exist, but they all lack one thing in comparison to Christianity. They are not falsifiable. That is, their truthfulness does not depend on any verifiable facts.

The incarnation also marks a difference between Christianity and all other world religions. God came into time and space. He verified this by miracles and by rising from the dead. All other religions make spiritual claims. Their human founders claim they have the way, yet their claims remain claims. Jesus didn't claim to be the Son of God and to have the power to forgive sins without offering supporting evidence in the face of unbelief. John records these words of Jesus: "I did tell you, but you do not believe. The miracles I do in My Father's name speak for Me" (John 10:25); "Even though you do not believe Me, believe the miracles, that you may know and understand that the Father is in Me, and I in the Father" (John 10:38). On one occasion Jesus claimed to forgive the sins of a paralytic (Mark 2:12). When the religious elite questioned His authority to do so, Jesus responded by restoring the boy's ability to walk. He performed this miracle in order to testify to His divine authority. The miracles of Jesus, and in particular His resurrection, separate Christianity from other religions today.

12. To what do the Scriptures testify?

13. Jesus' resurrection from the dead proves the Christian revelation (Acts 17:31). Nevertheless, mere acceptance of historical facts excludes a personal trust in the death and resurrection of Jesus for us. How do we become certain that these events took place for us? How do we become enlightened to this spirituality?

14. The death and resurrection give us certainty of God's love for human beings. God graciously continues to assure us of His love for us. Through what means does God continue to remind us of our salvation won in Christ's death?

Words
to Remember

I pray also that the eyes of your heart may be enlightened in order that you may know the hope to which He has called you, the riches of His glorious inheritance. Ephesians 1:18

Voice from Beyond

A man shakes and sobs. His sister's eyes well up with tears. The family just received wonderful news. Their mother is okay after all.

Four months earlier, while the surgeons operated on their mother, they waited anxiously in the hospital emergency room. When news of her death came, it crushed them. Uncertain of what comes after death, they visited a psychic for help. The message the psychic shared with them was just what they wanted to hear. They finally knew that their mother was in a better place.

Psychic mediums have received a lot of media attention. This story and similar ones are prevalent on televised psychic readings. John Edward, a contemporary psychic following in the tradition of Uri Geller, Shirley McLaine, and James Van Praagh, recently wrote a *New York Times* bestseller, appeared on *Larry King Live* and *Dateline*, and has his own weekly television show on the Sci-Fi Network. Edward claims that his work as a medium is a gift from God. According to him, God is a force whose energy allows him (and other psychics) to create their own psychic energy, whereby they are able to communicate with those who have "crossed over." He claims to use this gift in order to heal people grieving the deaths of loved ones. By speaking with relatives and friends who have "crossed over" to a different reality, he assures the grievers that life and death are part of a continuous cycle.

15. Have you ever seen or heard of psychic mediums? Reflect on the rising popularity of such spiritual advisors. Do you think their work offers genuine help to those needing spiritual advice? Explain.

16. Compare and contrast Edward's god to the Christian God. Compare and contrast the different views of life and death.

The Christian God is a personal being as opposed to an impersonal force or energy. The God revealed in Scripture desires a relationship with humanity and creation. Though He is everywhere in creation, He is not part of creation. In classic Christian spirituality, a sharp distinction remains between God and humans. Humans are subject to God in Christian thought, whereas psychic thought places humans and God as equals.

17. Christians often seek advice from their pastor. Can a Christian maintain a Christian worldview while seeking and trusting spiritual advice from a psychic?

Voices from Beyond?

Psychologists have analyzed respected and famous psychics. Their research demonstrates the deception that lies behind the psychic industry. Research shows that psychic mediums masterfully take advantage of the human psychology of belief.

Generally speaking, clients of psychic mediums find psychic readings edifying and applicable because they already believe in the medium's ability to contact the dead. Research indicates that clients tend to fit the broadest psychic reading into anticipated results. James E. Alcock, a psychologist from York University, remarks that mediums may offer completely generalized readings. Nonetheless, someone who already trusts in a psychic will accept the readings as personal and genuine. Astonishment and vulnerability increase for someone who has suffered the loss of a loved one. Psychics know that a grieving family member will welcome any supposed positive news from a deceased loved one.

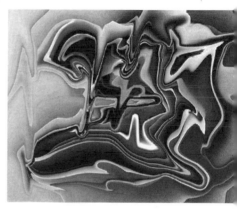

Beginning with supposed premonitions from the dead, mediums rattle off a list of names, colors, diseases, and so forth until they receive a "hit." Once an audience member or a client acknowledges that something from the list is familiar, such as a name or disease, the reading begins.

Some televised psychics appear convincing. However, it should be remembered that what you see on television is the edited version. After years of analysis, researchers have classified psychic readings into three categories. More often than not, the following reading techniques are utilized and are fairly easy to spot.

Hot readings obtain information on subjects ahead of time. For public readings, some mediums plant their own people in the audience in order to gather information from their conversations either before or during the session. Private readings use information from prior conversations with the client. For example, when someone sets up an appointment with a personal psychic, the psychic will often ask what the appointment involves. By the time the appointment takes place, the psychic has a good idea about the cares and concerns of the client. Clients typically forget what they told the psychic when they made the appointment.

Warm readings either feed off of hot readings or use psychological principles that apply to most people. For example, many people who have experienced the death of a spouse keep a token of remembrance from that person (e.g., the *Today Show*'s Katie Couric wore her husband's wedding band around her neck after her husband died). Psychics take advantage of these situations. They may say, "That ring on your necklace; it belonged to a loved one, didn't it?" Psychics learn through other subtle hints such as body language, which they use in order to pry information out of a person.

Cold readings are perhaps the most convincing of all psychic readings. They are made without any prior knowledge or acquaintance with a person/client. These usually take place in an audience with many members. The psychic will usually begin by "reading" the entire group, making fast statements such as "I'm getting an 'S-name'; it could be a man or woman, a spouse or sibling." After getting head nods from the audience, the psychic stops and probes a little further. "Is it a Steve, Scott, or Sarah?" You can imagine how many people in a large group know a Steve, Scott, or Sarah. From there, the psychic continues to probe for more hits.

Most psychics are uncomfortable with cold reads because they involve the most guesswork. For example, one researcher from *Skeptic Magazine* reviewed tapes of John Edward's cold readings. He concluded that Edward's accuracy was about 10 percent, even after editing.

Time magazine also investigated episodes of John Edward's psychic television show, *Crossing Over*. A review compared an actual public reading to the edited version for television, showing that Edward manipulated reads through editing to boost his accuracy rate. Producers used small portions of the original reading to patch together a thirty-minute, credible show, complete with commercials to break up inconsistencies. Imagine if you could take a live two-hour football game and edit it down to less than thirty minutes. You could tailor the results to reflect well on your favorite team. This is what John Edward does. He takes the highlights of his tapings and edits them into a clean, believable program.

Historians report that the famed magician Harry Houdini sought out a reliable psychic medium for years. His experience in magic and illusions enabled him to detect the most sophisticated of frauds. He went to the most reliable psychics he could find, but he always determined the psychics' tricks. Hence, Houdini was never able to find a reliable psychic.

Though many psychics claim their spiritual advice is for entertainment purposes, some claim that they are, in fact, connecting with spirits of the dead. Some appear very accurate on television.

18. List some possible explanations for a televised psychic's accuracy.

19. Psychics often, if not always, speak of the dead as those who have "passed on" or "crossed over." What worldview do these phrases indicate? What questions arise regarding the viability of such a worldview?

20. What problems are there in the psychic's claim to be gifted with abilities from God?

Logically speaking, a medium's claim to speak with the dead is either true or false. The psychic really divines the dead or he does not. If not, he is a charlatan. Though debunking popular mediums does not prove difficult, the possibility remains that some mediums make contact with spirits.

21. What dangers may be involved if mediums really contact the dead?

Words That Condemn

Psychics typically view death as a crossing over from one reality to the next. Hence, there is no heaven or hell. Regardless of one's faith or lack thereof, psychics such as John Edward assure relatives of their deceased loved one's security. There is no need for a Savior in this line of spiritual thought. A person simply transfers from one reality to the next. However, classic Christian spirituality tells a different story.

22. How does Jesus' death and the events that followed inform us about life and death?

Consulting spirits of the dead (necromancy) is expressly forbidden in the Old Testament. Necromancers and those who consulted necromancers were, under the old covenant, subject to the death penalty. Why such harsh consequences? The Old Testament recounts tale after tale of Israel's rejection of the true and living God. Israel continually adapted spiritual trends from their neighbors and consequently turned from worship of the one true God to the spurious and false gods of their neighbors.

The author of 1 Samuel records the story of King Saul consulting a medium (28:1–20). Learning of God's plan to give David the throne of Israel, Saul's jealous anger caused David to flee Israel. Though David had ample opportunity to take Saul's throne, he waited patiently for the Lord to fulfill His promise (16:1, 13). Aware of his impending doom, Saul turned to a medium for advice (15:26, 28). Then, looking for a way out, he requested to consult with Samuel.

23. Read the story of Saul and the Witch of Endor in 1 Samuel 28:1–20. Saul asked Samuel how to defeat the Philistines (28:15). What was Samuel's response?

24. Why did Saul seek out a medium even after he expelled mediums from Israel years earlier (28:3)? What does Samuel's response in verses 16–19 say about what God reveals through His prophets? What lessons regarding revelation apart from God's Word can be drawn from Samuel's response?

Consulting psychics turns our reliance from the certainty of God's mercy to the uncertainty of man's spiritual whims. However, we may turn our allegiance away from God in numerous ways. We doubt and turn our back on God when we seek answers from spiritual or earthly philosophy contrary to God's Word. Whether it favors a psychic medium or our own abilities, the sinful heart continually doubts God and His Word.

Think back to the account of Adam and Eve in the Garden of Eden. When the devil appeared to Eve in the form of a serpent, what was the first thing he asked Eve? "Did God really say . . . ?" As the story continues, Eve doubted God's command about fruit from the tree in the middle of the garden. Adam followed suit. Here lies the origin of sin and death—doubting God's warning and care.

St. Paul explains the consequences of Adam and Eve's disobedience. "Sin entered the world through one man, and death through sin, and in this way death came to all men" (Romans 5:12). Doubting God's Word leads to sin and death.

Though many psychic mediums prove false, Scripture informs us that necromancy is sometimes real. The National Spiritualist Association of Churches claims that the Bible endorses spiritism (necromancy).

When faced with competing spiritual truth claims, theologians from St. Paul to Martin Luther to C. S. Lewis have asked: "How do these views interact with what Jesus said about Himself and His work?" This question helps sort out the spiritual implications of a belief or practice.

Modern spiritism denies the person and work of Christ. Many psychics view Jesus as equivalent to any other man. Some may claim that He was more enlightened spiritually than normal man. However,

psychics believe that the same power that Jesus was able to tap into remains available to all people because all people share in the same psychic divine energy. Concerning Christ's work, many psychics reject Christ's atoning death on the cross. There is no sin and eternal damnation in psychic thought—and, hence, no need for a Savior.

25. In view of the contradictions between spiritism and Christianity, how do some Christians appeal to both beliefs? (For example, Jean Dixon, a noted psychic, was also a practicing Roman Catholic.)

The One
from the Dead

Perhaps our greatest fear is our fear of death. In
spite of our advances in science and medicine,
death appears undefeatable. Most people who seek
psychic mediums do so in order to be assured of
their loved one's fate.

26. What spiritual advice can a Christian give to those who fear
death? Explain how and why Christianity's answers to life after death
are the only certain answers.

Throughout the history of His people, God has revealed Himself
and His will to man. Immediately after the fall, God promised to
crush the work of Satan (Genesis 3:15). God restated this promise
throughout the history of Israel. Speaking through the Old Testament
prophets, God foretold the way in which He was going to redeem creation from death.

As Old Testament history unfolded, specific details of God's
agent of redemption were revealed. Finally, a baby was born in the
town of Bethlehem, as foretold by the prophet Micah. This baby was
the one appointed by God who would bring about His promised
redemption.

Indeed, this was no ordinary baby. In the flesh of this boy was
God Himself. Three decades into Jesus' life, God fulfilled the ancient
promise given from the beginning. Jesus—the God-man—went to the
cross. By substituting His righteousness for man's unrighteousness,
Jesus crushed the work of Satan.

Jesus' resurrection from the dead finalized the redemption of
humankind. The consequence of sin, which He took upon Himself,
had no power over Him. Christ defeated death.

This isn't just a story or spiritual wishful thinking. Nor is it a
mysterious event that occurred in another realm of reality. Seeing,

hearing, and touching Jesus after His resurrection convinced the disciples of His divinity (1 John 1:1–4). The reality of the resurrected Christ overwhelmed the disciples. Many of them wound up paying the ultimate price as martyrs for testifying to this truth. The events of Jesus' death and resurrection shaped the spirituality of Christ's early disciples. It was these events that fulfilled God's promise of redemption, whereby humans truly have fellowship with God Almighty.

27. Speaking of the witness of Christ's early disciples, the author Paul Maier states, "Myths don't make martyrs." In regard to those who deny Jesus' resurrection from the dead, how does the martyrdom of the early disciples testify to the truth of Jesus' resurrection?

St. Paul argued that if Christ did not rise bodily from the dead, Christianity is useless and a false faith (1 Corinthians 15:14). Furthermore, Paul stated, "If only for this life we have hope in Christ, we are to be pitied more than all men" (verse 19). However, Christ rose from the dead. Therefore, we can be certain of our resurrection to eternal life.

During His lifetime Jesus raised people from the dead. However, these people eventually returned to death. Jesus is different. Forty days after His resurrection, He ascended into heaven. Jesus is the only authority on life after death. He is the only one who can speak of it with firsthand experience. Mediums may speak as if they are able to

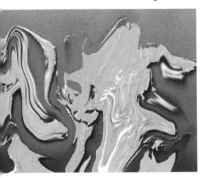

contact the dead. However, only Jesus can give conclusive answers regarding life after death. From eternity, He stepped into human time and space. Within the sphere of time and space He died and came back from the dead. He then ascended back into heaven to the right hand of God the Father. He alone is able to offer authoritative answers to our greatest fear. He alone is "the way and the truth and the life" (John 14:6).

28. Read 1 Corinthians 15:12–23. Paul states that death came through one man. Where do spiritual beliefs shaped by men lead? In whom do we have life?

29. What implications does Paul's argument in 1 Corinthians have for shaping our personal spirituality? Congregational spirituality?

Words
to Remember

J esus said . . . , "I am the resurrection and the life. He who believes in Me will live, even though he dies; and whoever lives and believes in Me will never die." John 11:25–26

Your Destiny

D onald Regan's book *For the Record* shocked Americans. The former chief of staff to Ronald Reagan reported that most of the president's appearances and actions were approved in advance by Mrs. Reagan's astrologer.

Astrology remains popular today. Horoscopes drawn from astrological readings appear in newspapers, in magazines, and on television. According to professional astrological organizations, there are more than 10,000 professional astrologers who serve 20 million clients.

The roots of astrology reach back to the second millennium B.C. Astrologers from the early civilizations of Babylonia developed horoscopes based on the position of stars and planets. These horoscopes predicted what would most likely happen from month to month. Babylonian astrologers also developed the signs of the zodiac—astrological categories based on twelve divisions in the sky. Each of the divisions were assigned a name drawn from the planets and constellations found within each sphere. The twelve signs of the zodiac correspond to twelve periods over the course of a year. Zodiacal signs (e.g., Scorpio, Libra, Virgo, Leo) were thought to determine personality traits and relational compatibility.

Once astrology made its way into Roman culture (a few centuries prior to the birth of Christ), astrologers fashioned horoscopes for individuals, much like today's horoscopes.

30. Name some popular places where horoscopes and astrological readings are found. What place does astrology hold in society? Do you think it has become an accepted part of American culture? Explain.

31. What logical, scientific, or moral difficulties might astrology pose? Does reading and relying on horoscopes present a problem for the Christian faith?

Science and the Stars

Horoscopes based on astrological readings pose a variety of difficulties. As discussed in chapter 1, historians have observed an increase in superstition when historic, traditional religions decline. Some contemporary astrologers argue that mathematical and scientific formulations confirm astrological predictions; however, scientific and logical analysis reveals problems with astrology.

According to the Committee for Scientific Investigation of the Claims of the Paranormal, rigorous scientific tests have discounted the claims of astrologers. For example, a test was conducted on more than 3,000 astrological predictions. Only 10 percent proved to be reasonably accurate.

In an attempt to rescue the reputation of astrology, supporters claim that among the many frauds there still remain a few authentic astrologers. This raises the question "How do you know which astrologer to trust?" The astrologer typically answers, "The one whose readings come true."

Another scientific investigation showed the difficulty of resting astrology's legitimacy on experimental proof. A researcher took out an advertisement in a French newspaper. The advertisement promised a detailed, 10-page horoscope for free. Approximately 150 people sent in their zodiacal information. The researcher responded to all the inquiries by sending them the horoscope of a serial murderer. He enclosed a questionnaire with the horoscope asking for the accuracy of the astrological reading. Ninety-four percent of the inquirers claimed the readings were accurate for them! Ninety percent shared the positive results with friends and family.

Where science sheds light on astrology's inconsistencies, logical analysis points out a fallacy in reason. Astrologers who devise horoscopes do so on the basis of the 12 zodiac signs. Horoscopes given in the newspaper, on television, or through personal readings do so on the basis of 12 zodiacal divisions in the sky. This begs the question "What are the reasons or grounds for dividing the sky in such a way?" Some contemporary astrologers argue for anywhere between 8 and 24 zodiac divisions in the sky. How could we know which zodiacal scheme is the correct one? What guarantees that the stars or a person's zodiacal sign really contains information about one's life? These and other questions remain unanswered.

The historical roots of astrology reveal another major problem with the system. Astronomical research shows that when the signs of the zodiac were established, the constellations in each division were different than today. Science has shown that in the last 2,000 years constellations have shifted 30 degrees. The constellations that determined the zodiacal divisions moved over to the next division. Where Virgo was found 2,000 years ago, Leo is now located.

32. Ten percent of astrological predictions were not discredited by the Committee for Scientific Investigation of the Claims of the Paranormal. What could account for their accuracy?

33. Supporters of astrology claim that in spite of the charlatans, genuine astrologers still remain. What doubts might you have about alleged genuine astrologers?

Walter Truett Anderson, author of *Reality Isn't What It Used to Be*, comments that astrology and horoscopes appear to be the national religion of Americans.

34. What do you think Anderson means? Do you agree or disagree? Why or why not?

All religious and philosophical systems of thought follow some sort of authority. For example, Muslims follow the authority of the Qur'an, and a rationalist follows the authority of reason and experience. The authority one follows typically prescribes one's view of reality and truth (worldview).

35. What is astrology's ultimate authority? What is the worldview of an astrologer? Is a worldview that incorporates astrology compatible with the Christian worldview? Explain.

As noted above, historians have observed a culture's movement toward superstition when traditional and historic religious thought declines. An early twentieth-century Christian writer, G. K. Chesterton, argued that superstitious and arbitrary spirituality is dull. Meanwhile, a Christian spirituality that wrestles with the tension between faith and reason is difficult, yet exciting and the only guarantee of sanity.

36. What do you think G. K. Chesterton meant? Compare and contrast classic Christian spirituality with contemporary astrological spirituality.

Stars and Scarecrows

The prophet Jeremiah warned God's people against associating with foreign religious practices such as astrology. Jeremiah compared the practice of astrology to the absurdity of worshiping a wooden idol carved from a tree. He also compared trust and fear of astrological signs to revering a scarecrow in a melon patch.

37. Read Jeremiah 10:2–5. What characteristic do the stars in the sky share with wood from a tree? Why does Jeremiah compare reverence for "signs in the sky" to the worship of man-made idols?

38. Why do you think the prophets warned ancient Israel about falling into the religious practices of other cultures?

Astrology presented serious moral difficulties for ancient Israel. Just as Christians today are surrounded by a variety of religious opinions, the Israelites were surrounded by cultures that practiced astrology, among other pagan rites. Moses warned the Israelites not to place their trust in created things on earth or in the heavens (Deuteronomy 4:15–19). To do so would provoke God's wrath (v. 24).

In the New Testament, St. Paul repeated the command not to trust in created things. He argued that those who follow the authority of created things such as stars and planets are in spiritual bondage (Galatians 4:3).

Following the authority of astrological signs and astrologers breaks the First Commandment. Although astrologers and their clients break the First Commandment, all of humanity violates this law as well. Our human nature entices us to trust and worship gods other than the one true God. Astrology and horoscopes are symptoms of an idolatrous heart, and all people share this same condition.

It is our nature to turn from God toward ourselves and other created things for temporal blessings and eternal salvation (Romans 1:25). Our actual and visible sin is not the fundamental problem; it's who we are as children of Adam—children born cursed under the Law.

39. The First Commandment teaches us to have God first in our lives: to fear, love, and trust in God above all things. How is fearing God different from fearing the destiny forecast by astrologers?

When astrology made its way into Roman culture, the planets and constellations within the zodiacal divisions were worshiped as individual gods. The sixteenth-century church reformer Martin Luther noted that the Romans worshiped these "gods" because they desired the attributes associated with them. For example, Mercury was worshiped and trusted for wealth and prosperity. To have this god on your side guaranteed your success.

40. Does trusting in God imply that Christians can "take it easy" in their careers, schoolwork, or family life? Are Christians *destined* for success? What does it mean to trust solely in God for daily provisions and blessings while maintaining a strong work ethic and Christian lifestyle?

41. Can astrology and horoscopes coincide with Christian spirituality? Explain.

"Sign" of Salvation

A philosopher said that if you accept astrology, you have to accept that you are a born loser or a born winner. Astrology maintains a deterministic worldview. That is, human fate is already predetermined. The choices that humans make have already been made for them. A person's zodiacal sign determines his or her fate.

42. How does Christ's death on the cross and God's universal mission to all people inform us of fate and predestination?

The Gospel of Matthew records the visit of the Magi from the East to Jerusalem (Matthew 2:1–12). Though little is known about the Magi, they were most likely wealthy astronomers/astrologers or magicians from the area of Persia. Something extraordinary drew them to Jerusalem. Some sort of unusual sign in the sky appeared, which aroused their curiosity. So they followed this "star" (the Greek word for star can refer to any celestial body apart from the sun).

Upon their arrival in Jerusalem, the Magi asked, "Where is the one who has been born king of the Jews? We saw His star in the east and have come to worship Him" (v. 2). After King Herod heard of the Magi's request, he asked the Jewish scholars and priests where this king was to be born. From the book of the prophet Micah, written about seven hundred years prior to this event, the Scribes were able to point to Bethlehem, the city where the "king of the Jews"—the promised Messiah—was to be born.

When the Magi finally made it to the place where Jesus was born, they "bowed down and worshipped" Him (v. 11). What prompted rich, Gentile Wise Men from the East to bow down and worship this infant? The promise given right after the fall of Adam and Eve (Genesis 3:15) and repeated throughout Israel's history was to be fulfilled in this child. The shepherd of God's people (Matthew 2:6 and Micah 5:2)—all people—had come.

43. When the Magi asked where the "king of the Jews" was to be born, where did the Jewish scholars go for their answer? What does this say about where we are to find certainty about God, our life, and eternal life?

44. In the example of the Magi, is Christianity viewed as a religion bound by cultural walls, or does it transcend such boundaries? Explain. What are the implications for your understanding?

Three decades after the Magi visited Jesus, He was put to death on a cross and then rose from His grave. His death paid the debt for sin, and His resurrection certified the destruction of the work of Satan and the consequences of sin—death.

Christ's death shows the consequence of our sinful nature. It took more than a cursory show of spirituality and good deeds by humans to reverse the effects of sin. No amount of religious piety or godly living could change our natural inclination towards sin and outright rebellion against God. (Good works and piety for the purpose of meriting God's favor are, in fact, a form of self-idolatry.) The effects of our sinful nature were not reversible by human efforts. Only the death of God's Son could reverse the judgment for a sinful humanity. The resurrection of Christ validates the victory won in the death of Christ. It certifies the destruction of sin, death, and Satan's stronghold over us.

Following the sign of a bright star, receiving the certain location from the Scripture, the Magi were led to an infant child. In a manger laid the Savior of humankind. God's mission in the world extends to all people. The star the Magi followed led to the Scriptures, and the Scriptures told of the Savior's birth. In the Scriptures we find Christ. In Christ all people find salvation.

Words
to Remember

B ut now a righteousness from God, apart from law, has been made known, to which the Law and the Prophets testify. This righteousness from God comes through faith in Jesus Christ to all who believe. Romans 3:21–22

Contemplate

W hat do Electroencelography (EEG),
Computerized Axial Tomography (CAT),
Magnetic Resonance Imaging (MRI), Single
Photon Emission Computed Tomography (SPECT),
and Positron Emission Tomography (PET) have to do
with spirituality? As of late, quite a bit.

Work begun by the late Dr. Eugene d'Aquili of
the University of Pennsylvania's medical school
opened up fascinating avenues for scientific research
into how the brain functions during religious experiences. Dr. d'Aquili and his colleague Dr. Andrew
Newberg have observed neurological changes in the
brain during meditative states.

Their research has developed into a new science called *neurotheology*. This science explores links between spirituality and the human
brain. During a recent interview with *Reader's Digest*, Newberg
remarked that man's idea of a "higher reality" might actually be real.
The interviewer asked Newberg what he meant by "real." He responded that the existence of a higher reality might be as real as a table.
Such a thing, Newberg continued, is definitely not inconsistent with
science. The interviewer asked Newberg if such a thing is observable
in a scientific way. Newberg responded that it is. According to neurotheology, observations and pictures of the brains of Buddhist monks
and Franciscan nuns during meditative states demonstrate the human
ability to connect to a higher reality.

Though westerners often view meditation and contemplation as
an eastern religious practice, Christian mystics from the early Middle
Ages engaged in contemplation/meditation as well. In fact, medieval
clergy were distinguished as either "contemplative" or "secular." The
goal of Christian mysticism was to achieve a unity with God, a mysti-

cal union. The world's great religions share a common tradition of meditation or contemplation.

45. Do you know anyone who practices meditation actively? What are his or her reasons? Read and reflect on Psalm 1:2.

46. Had you been present at the interview with Newberg, what questions would you have asked him?

47. What are some positive aspects of meditation? Negative aspects?

Science
and God

Using sophisticated scientific tools, Newberg's research found that during meditative states the human brain is deprived of neural information necessary to distinguish between the self and the external world. Thus, he concludes, while a person is meditating, he or she experiences a union with God and/or a "higher reality."

The research pursued in neurotheology falls within the realm of

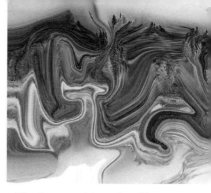

science. The research tools used and the experimental method all fall within the realm of science as well. Yet conclusions drawn from neurotheological research step outside the bounds or limits of practical science. In effect, the science makes a leap from observation of certain neurological activity to statements about humans and their connection to God, something that lies outside the scope of scientific observation.

The faults of neurotheological research lie not in experiments and observations, but rather in its theological conclusions. Here's why. Science typically reasons inductively. Observations from various experiments provide hard scientific data. Upon establishing all the evidence, scientists interpret what the evidence means. That is, from the evidence a scientist reaches a conclusion.

Newberg's tests observed monks during meditation and nuns at prayer. Using a SPECT (Single Photon Emission Computed Tomography), scientists took pictures of the blood flow in each subject's brain. After studying the pictures, scientists noticed that the left parietal lobe of the brain showed a steady decrease in blood flow as the subject reached a spiritual peak. The left parietal lobe is responsible for distinguishing between the self and external reality. By these experiments, science has discovered a neural-physiological explanation for the interconnectedness that Buddhist monks feel and the mystical union that Christian mystics feel. However, Newberg attempts to go further. Using the same evidence, he infers that these religious experiences are more than a feeling. He claims this is evidence of a higher reality.

Although scientists are able to observe changes in neural activity during a meditative state, they are unable to observe God or a higher reality. When neurotheologians claim that meditation or any other religious experience actually connects one with God or a higher reality, they step outside the bounds of scientific observation. True, certain neurological activities occur when someone meditates; this is observable. It does not follow that someone who meditates or engages in contemplative prayer is actually connecting with a higher reality or even God.

From a scientific perspective, the idea that religious experience makes a man aware that he is connected with the divine is shown to be nothing more than neurological processes in the brain. Thus, when the statement is made that man is able to connect with a higher reality through meditation and prayer, science shows that it is only the decrease in neurological activity that causes man to *feel* he is so connected.

The claim that meditation or prayer connects one to God has certain theological problems as well; namely, how would one know he or she is in fact connecting with God? Can feelings identify the God we pray to? The world's religions have different views about God. The variety of contradictory definitions and ideas about God show how difficult it is to pin down the true God on the basis of religious experience. Which religious experience is really connecting with the true God? What about other religious experiences? Could they be hallucinations? Theologians have been pondering these questions for centuries. Because of the limits to human knowledge regarding God, the only knowledge of God that we can achieve is that which God gives or reveals to us. All other knowledge is speculative at best.

48. What assumptions does neurotheology make? What are the problems with these assumptions?

49. Philosophers and theologians have devised elaborate proofs for God's existence. Are you familiar with any? Explain. Though he does not claim to offer foolproof evidence for God's existence, Newberg claims that neurotheology may add evidence of God's existence. What do you think?

50. Arguments for God's existence fall in the realm of what is called natural theology. What are some positive aspects of natural theology? Negative? What can natural theology tell us about God?

Different Gospels
Be Damned

Meditation and contemplative prayer often invoke deeply religious experiences. These experiences can excite or calm us. Feeling personally connected to God or a higher reality charges our spiritual fervor. Spiritual experiences offer an exciting substitute to life's mundane activities. Some find such religious experience a thrilling alternative to traditional religious practices. Nevertheless, we should examine where religious experiences lead us.

During religious experiences, our feelings tell us that we have connected to a higher reality. Newberg's research informs us that this is the result of neurological processes in the brain. Yet the experience feels so real. Perhaps it is.

Scientific evidence is unable to prove or disprove authentic spiritual encounters with God or a higher reality. However, the experience itself may give some indication of the value of religious experience. Practices such as deep meditation and contemplative prayer begin on human initiative. As these experiences intensify, feelings of spiritual awareness arise. People feel a connection or a communion with something bigger than themselves. This mystical union or interconnectedness cannot be described. They "just know" that they experienced something deeply religious.

Some call the thing or essence encountered in religious experiences "God." Others call it a "higher reality." Mystics of all stripes offer a variety of descriptive and nondescriptive names. Here lies the problem with religious experience.

Terms like "higher reality" and "God" suggest a sort of anonymity found in religious experiences. A connection or union to something bigger than us may be perceived. But what is it? Does this higher reality or God have a name? Is it the God of the Bible? Because religious experience is so personal, it is difficult and perhaps impossible to arrive at universal descriptive terms. By its very nature, religious experience can only lead to an unknown God.

An unknown God is a safe God. Religious experiences can lead us to the God *we want to find*. However, God revealed Himself in history in no uncertain terms.

51. Read Exodus 19:3–25. Moses had an intense religious experience. How did the rest of the Israelites know that Moses was in fact receiving revelations from God? How would you describe Moses' experience?

52. On Mount Sinai, what did God reveal about Himself and His relationship with His people?

Throughout the history of Israel, God revealed Himself in terms of rules and promises (Law and Gospel). Every time Israel disobeyed God's commandments, God disciplined them. However, God's grace was quick to follow. God constantly reminded the Israelites that they were "a kingdom of priests and a holy nation" (19:6). Through the nation of Israel, the Messiah was to come. This Messiah, God promised, would be a blessing to all nations. The Messiah publicly displayed the Good News of forgiveness of sins. The Law of God was fulfilled in the Gospel of Jesus.

The unknown God of religious experiences is often foreign to the God who revealed Himself in history. Genuine religious experience encounters God as He reveals Himself in Law and Gospel.

Where the Law reveals the gap between humans and God, the Gospel builds a bridge across the gap. God's revelation of the Gospel came in the person of Jesus Christ. According to the apostles who lived with Jesus and witnessed His resurrection, the forgiveness of sins in the Gospel of Jesus offers the only genuine religious experience.

However, reports of spiritual experiences during meditative states and contemplative prayer are often quite distant from the Gospel. Saint Paul offers specific ways for distinguishing between misleading and genuine religious experiences. "Even if we or an angel from heaven should preach a gospel other than the one we preached to you, let him be eternally condemned! As we already said, so now I say again: If anybody is preaching to you a gospel other than what you accepted, let him be eternally condemned!" (Galatians 1:8–9).

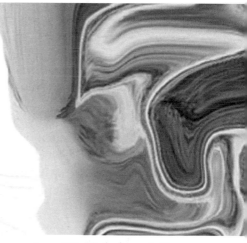

Let's apply this specifically to the religious experiences covered above. God's revelation to man is identified in the Law and Gospel. An experience of God's Law condemns humans. The Gospel brings humans into union with God. The Gospel is found in the person of Jesus. The unity with God found in religious experience must identify with Jesus Christ. Apart from Christ, it is a different gospel, "which is really no gospel at all" (Galatians 1:7). Different gospels be damned.

53. What could religious experiences apart from an experience of the biblical Christ be attributed to?

54. Different churches offer a variety of worship styles. In an attempt to appeal to different people, many churches advertise new and fresh worship *experiences*. Regardless of whether a historic liturgy is used or a contemporary style of worship, what should always be considered as Christians choose their style of worship?

Free to Experience the Gospel

The sixteenth-century church reformer Martin Luther spent his youthful days in meditation and prayer. Luther chose a contemplative life. But his attempt to find union with God resulted in self-inflicted injuries. Luther refrained from food for long periods of time, whipped his body, and slept on a cold stone floor. In spite of his efforts, Luther's conscience could not be eased. No amount of meditation and prayer, acts of penance, or good deeds satisfied Luther. He was sure of his separation from God because he could not do what was right.

Luther's anxiety resulted from the self-awareness of his unrighteousness. He experienced the demands of the Law. Luther knew full well that he could not stand before his righteous Creator. The demands of the Law and God's justice kept man from union with God.

But in the Scripture, Luther learned the Gospel of the forgiveness of sins and righteousness before God. He saw that man's sin and alienation before God were placed upon Jesus at the cross. God reconciled the world to Himself through the death of His Son.

As Luther continued to contemplate the cross, he asked how this reconciliation could become his own. He found the answer once again in Scripture: "The righteous will live by faith" (Romans 1:17). Righteousness before God comes through faith. A simple trust in the merits of Christ unites people to the righteousness of Christ—a righteousness that assures them of their right standing before God.

55. What about you? What led you to the cross of Christ?

The wonder of the Gospel is not that we can reach God through meditation or some other form of religious experience. Instead, God has reached out to us through His Son, Jesus. Religion is not spiritual hide-and-seek, with us groping after God. We can know Him because He made Himself known in Christ! (John 1:18).

We often associate meditation or contemplative prayer with eastern religions, which emphasize "emptying" the mind. However, as we see in the example of Luther, Christian meditation and/or contemplation is not a noncognitive, mind emptying practice. Christian meditation is full of content (Psalm 1:2). Luther wrote that true knowledge of God comes from "prayer, meditation, and fear of God." The Scriptures and the person of Christ are the proper objects and source of Christian meditation and contemplation. God reveals Himself here. Here we truly encounter God.

During Christian worship, God comes to us in the gifts of grace—the Gospel and the Sacraments. In the reading and preaching of God's Word, we experience God as He reveals Himself. When the pastor announces the absolution, we experience the forgiveness of sins as if spoken by Christ Himself. During Holy Communion we feed on the very body and blood of Christ. God invites us to an intimate, personal union with Him in the eating and drinking of Christ's body and blood. The Word and Sacraments assure us of an authentic religious experience. We can be sure that in this we are united with the one true God because He instituted these practices Himself.

Like Luther in the sixteenth century, the promise of authentic religious experience is available in the twenty-first century. Meditating on Christ's death and contemplating the Gospel in the Holy Scriptures, we experience the forgiveness of sins. Every Sunday God invites us to experience forgiveness in a tangible way. With the bread and wine of Holy Communion, we partake in the body and blood of Jesus Christ. In God's Word and the Sacraments we find God as He reveals Himself—in the forgiveness of sins.

56. The psalmist wrote, "I rise before dawn and cry for help; I have put my hope in Your word. My eyes stay open through the watches of the night, that I may meditate on Your promises" (Psalm 119:147–148). When faced with the turmoil of life, where can we go for hope?

57. Where does all authentic religious experience begin and end? Compare this to popular notions of religious experience.

Words
to Remember

May the words of my mouth and the meditation of my heart be pleasing in Your sight, O LORD, my Rock and my Redeemer. Psalm 19:14

CHAPTER FIVE

Magickal Mystery

T he Harry Potter books, the film *The Craft*, the television program *Sabrina the Teenage Witch*, the game Magic: the Gathering. American popular culture contains hints of the ancient pagan religions of pre-Christian Europe. Modern sorcerers, witches, and warlocks claim to trace their ancestry from this era.

In 1974 various groups of witches formed the American Council of Witches. Since then, the popularity of Wiccanism continues to grow. Witches establish covens on college and high school campuses. For example, in Cleveland, witches, vampires, and werewolves rent themselves out to  liven up parties. Television shows feature attractive witches and gallant vampires endowed with magical abilities. Seeking empowerment, feminists and environmentalists worship Mother Earth and the goddesses of Wicca.

The predominant practice of Wiccanism is some form of magick (not to be confused with the stage performance of magic). In their ceremonies and rites, Wiccans attempt to master supernatural forces. Spells, charms, and other magical techniques alter the course of natural events. Witches use white magick to help others and black magick to do harm. Wiccanism offers power and rebellion against traditional religion and science.

58. Have you ever heard of or encountered anyone involved with magick and/or Wiccanism? Explain. What media attention has Wiccanism received in your area?

59. Daniel Cohen, author of *A Natural History of Unnatural Things*, observes that witchcraft has not yet been taken seriously. Why do you think Wiccanism is largely overlooked?

Magick, Drugs, Sex, and Psychosis

When we think of witches, visions come to mind of ugly old women riding on broomsticks accompanied by a black cat. The Middles Ages saw a rise in witchcraft. This was suppressed by the infamous witch hunts of the sixteenth and seventeenth centuries. However, modern day witches and warlocks resemble the status quo of society. New converts to Wiccanism often are naïve about the depths of its occultic involvement. Yet much of Wiccanism threatens the mental and physical health of those involved.

At the center of Wiccan activity lies its practice of magick. White and black magick rites deceive those involved. Research has demonstrated a high correlation between Wiccanism, occultism, and schizophrenia. Constant practice and self-persuasion of the reality of white or black magick causes a loss of the human ability to distinguish between reality and illusion. An expert in family counseling, Kurt E. Koch, confirms this theory. In detailed case studies he demonstrates the adverse effects that Wiccanism and occultism have on families.

Daniel Cohen notes that witchcraft has a definite connection to drug use and sexual deviancy. In many cases, drug use and sexual promiscuity are encouraged during Wiccan rituals. The American Council of Witches formally states that sex is a symbol of power, the embodiment of life, and a source of energy used in magickal practices and religious worship.

Accounts of the infamous black magick champion Aleister Crowley tell of excessive drug use and ritualistic sacrifices. Police departments around America record case after case of drug-induced deaths resulting from magick rituals. More than a few murders have been traced back to black magick cults. Santoria (practiced by some African-Americans and Hispanics) and Satanism (practiced by some Caucasians) employ blood sacrifices. Traces of animal sacrifices offered to Mother Earth or Satan are common finds in areas where witchcraft is practiced. In some cases, evidence of human sacrifice has been found. However, Wiccans officially distance themselves from such activities and insist they do not practice Satanism.

In 2001 the Waupan Correctional Institution in Wisconsin offered Jamyi Witch, a Wiccan priestess, a position as a prison chaplain. After this was reported in the media, the public protested. The case went to trial. After all the psychiatric evidence and police reports were heard, it was deemed unsafe to have a witch as a chaplain. The scientific and legal evidence was so strong that the state could not risk having a Wiccan counsel prison inmates.

Though some witches claim that Wiccanism is innocent, the evidence shows otherwise. Certainly there are Wiccan fads that pass with little harm. However, serious involvement in Wiccanism and magick arts tells a different story.

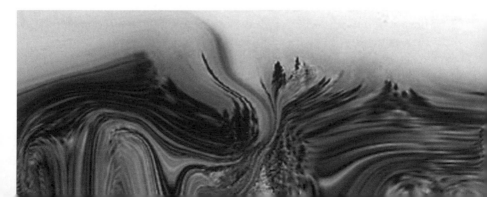

60. Apart from naturalistic explanations, what could account for psychological problems in witches?

61. What are some dangers that result from the slightest involvement with magick rites?

Quest
for Power

B oth the Old and New Testaments make repeated references to sorcery and witchcraft and condemn their practice. For example, Luke recorded Paul's run-in with a sorcerer. Read Acts 13:6–10. This account gives us interesting insight into the work of Satan. The Jewish sorcerer Elymas was the proconsul's attendant. When the proconsul desired to hear the Word of the Lord, what did the sorcerer do? He tried to interfere with Paul and the proconsul. Satan accomplishes this interference in at least two ways. False religious teachings offer alternatives to the one and only true religion. These religions also claim to have overwhelming signs of their power. These signs seek to sway people away from God, as their power attests to some sort of spiritual authority.

62. In spite of Elymas's attempt to curtail God's Word, Paul exposes Elymas for who he is. Of what does Paul accuse him?

63. At first, Elymas's feats of magick convinced the proconsul of his spiritual authority. What does Paul do to convince the proconsul otherwise?

Like Paul's identification of Elymas's sorcery with Satan, Wiccanism and magick obtain their powers from the same source. Whatever powers a witch might display come from the devil. Satan uses these signs to deceive those who are seeking spiritual fulfillment.

At its heart, Wiccanism is a quest for power in the natural order and over other people. Wiccanism teaches man that he is his own god. Offering earthly riches and power through magick, Wiccanism teaches human autonomy. Reliance upon magick and false religious teaching offers no eternal hope.

64. Authorities during the Middle Ages used the Old Testament civil law to support their witch hunts. Drawing from verses like Exodus 22:18—"Do not allow a sorceress to live" medieval Europeans justified their murder of accused witches. Does this verse and others like it still apply? Why or why not?

Eternal Certainty

Using magic as a metaphor, the British author C. S. Lewis wrote *The Lion, the Witch and the Wardrobe* to paint an image of the suffering, death, and resurrection of Jesus. (During Lewis's lifetime, laws against witchcraft were lifted in England, giving rise to the Wicca movement in the 1950s.) In order to release a boy from the spell of a witch, the lion Aslan passively submits to humiliation and eventual death. Crushed after seeing Aslan die, the main characters fear that the witch's magic had overcome the lion. However, Aslan returned to life. The lion explained to the children that the witch's magic wasn't enough to overcome a deeper magic—a magic that turned the tables on death.

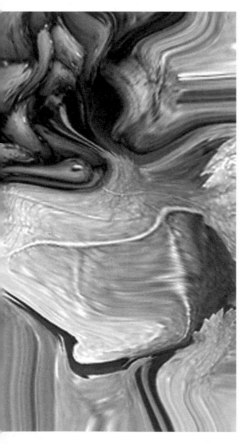

In this way, C. S. Lewis creatively pictured the teachings of the Gospel throughout his Chronicles of Narnia. Just as Aslan overcame death and reversed the curse of the witch, Jesus' death on the cross and resurrection from the dead overturned the curse of sin, death, and the devil.

Wiccans and those involved with magick claim to possess extraordinary power. In a society enthralled with the pursuit of power, we should not be surprised that witchcraft finds followers. Its spectacular claims arouse interest.

Nevertheless, we need not fear. Paul sets the example for those redeemed by Christ. Through the use of magick, the sorcerer at Paphos (Elymas) managed to acquire a position as the proconsul's attendant. When this sorcerer stood in the way of God's Word, Paul defied him. Attributing his show of power to God Himself, Paul blinded the sorcerer. With the sorcerer blinded and removed from the proconsul, Paul taught him about Jesus' authority over all things. Paul received power from the risen Jesus. This same power blinded the sorcerer. When faced with this power, the proconsul believed the Gospel.

Both Christians and neopagans should remember the superstition and fear that dominated Europe in pre-Christian times. For cultures that live in fear of spirits, witches, and witch doctors, the Gospel comes like a welcome light in the darkness. The Gospel has power. All the devil's powers could not defeat the crucified Jesus. He conquered all worldly and spiritual powers in His victorious resurrection from the dead.

He continues to reign over the powers of the devil. Baptism claimed us as Christ's own. Far from an empty ritual, the act of washing connected to the promises of God assures us of our protection from the powers of the devil. This assurance never waivers. We can stand certain in God's promise at Baptism.

Each week we see God's power at work in our midst. When we confess our sins before God, our pastors pronounce powerful words of absolution. These words—"in the stead and by the command of my Lord Jesus Christ I forgive you all your sins"—are God's words for us. We can rely on our right standing before God in Holy Absolution.

In spite of the dangers that witchcraft and magick present, we need not be afraid. We can be certain that the devil has no hold over us. Jesus' resurrection sealed and certified this promise.

65. Spend some time reviewing the nature, blessings, power, and significance of Baptism. Read Ezekiel 36:24–27 and Colossians 2:9–15.

66. Review the Office of the Keys and confession in Luther's Small Catechism. Read Matthew 16:13–19 and John 20:19–23.

67. Wiccanism expresses anger towards Christianity, largely due to the witch hunts of the early modern period and the Salem witch trials. What are some ways to bring the Gospel to somebody involved in Wiccanism?

Words
to Remember

You, dear children, are from God and have overcome them, because the one who is in you is greater than the one who is in the world. 1 John 4:4

CHAPTER SIX

Body and Mind

lternative approaches to healing have recently grown in popularity. Here are some examples:

Madonna and Sharon Stone swear by yoga. In addition to other celebrities, many college students and business professionals practice it. Although it began in India some 3,000 years before the time of Christ, yoga has found its way into American culture.

A woman feels tingles in her hand while holding a crystal. Having experienced foot pain for more than ten years, she decides to ask an expert on crystals how to use them. So she asks the salesman what will happen if she holds the crystal to her foot. When her foot heals, she believes that the crystal has healed it.

A television program films a Brazilian doctor performing lipoma (a lumpy, fatty deposit) removal on a patient. This doctor uses a rusty knife and no antiseptics or anesthetics, yet the patient feels no pain and receives a successful surgery. The surgeon's secret: a deceased German doctor has possessed him during the operation.

68. Evaluate the above scenarios. Do you think these health techniques contribute to a healthy lifestyle? Do you see positive aspects to them? Negative aspects?

Health and Science

M edical surveys show an increase in the growth of health and healing alternatives. Some of these alternatives contribute to mental and physical health. However, many threaten the physical and spiritual health of those involved.

For example, most people know of the benefits of stretching. Medical research widely documents that yoga helps decrease back pain and other sorts of bodily pain as well as relieving stress. Due to this, the general public considers yoga helpful, certainly not harmful. For the most part it is. Nevertheless, yoga practice and the philosophy behind yoga tell a different story.

The word *yoga* itself means a yoking together of mind, body, and soul. Just prior to the time of Christ, an eastern doctor and philosopher, Pantanjali, set down a list of eight rules that lead to fulfillment in yogic practice. This list is based on eastern religious assumptions and purposes. When followed, the yogi will find self-realization and oneness with the universe (*samadhi*). In other words, the religious aspects of yoga teach the monistic worldview described in chapter 1.

Eastern religions such as Buddhism and Hinduism and their American New Age counterparts teach that humans share in the oneness of the universe or are actually divine by nature. Self-realization awakens us to our oneness with the universe and our divinity.

69. Can a Christian practice yoga? Explain.

New "medical" practices provide alternative approaches to individual health. Though positive results are documented in some cases, practices such as crystal, aura, and psychic healings lack scientific explanation.

Crystals, for example, serve as good energy transmitters in elcctronics. They are used in watches, radios, computer chips, lasers, and so forth. Consequently, New Agers assume that they must also be good transmitters of energy in the body. However, scientific research is unable to substantiate this claim.

A popular New Age magazine, *Spirit Seeker*, claims that science verifies the existence of auras around humans. Aura healing takes place when a healer senses imbalances in a person's aura. New Age defines auras as a sort of force field around a person made up of positive and negative energies. Aura healers find the imbalance and set them aright. From what science can tell, human bodies have electrical charges. Whether these electrical charges act as a force field, science does not know.

Psychic surgeons claim to perform surgeries relying on their psychic senses alone. Whether deceased doctors possess psychic surgeons or surgeons work with their eyes shut, the American Medical Association warns against such practices! They are unable to verify accounts of psychic healing.

For many, alternative healing procedures appear real. However, these alternatives lack scientific evidence and long-term tests to verify their safety or reliability. The American Medical Association warns against relying upon them at all.

70. What do you think accounts for the attraction to alternative medicines?

71. Should all alternative medicines be abandoned? Explain.

72. What could be some dangers of relying upon crystals, psychics, or aura balancing for physical and mental health?

The Diagnosis

Former New Age believer Elliot Miller claims that powers of suggestion account for much of the alleged positive results from alternative healing. He and others do note some unexplained events, which seem to vindicate positive claims. Yet he and others are quick to point out that other powers beside psychic powers are at work.

Scripture does not inform us of psychic energy pervading the universe for use by humans. Nor does it inform us of a divine spark within or a oneness we share with all of reality. Scripture does inform us of a deceptive power at work in the universe. Satan works through whatever means possible to deceive God's creation. When people combine alternative health options with a nonbiblical worldview and then look to these practices for healing and other desired ends, the door is opened to deception.

Scripture informs us of the first of Satan's deceptions, from which all deceptions arose (Romans 5:12–14). Yet the choice belongs to man. The foolishness of human choices has been diagnosed. The indictment is clear. On account of sin, we have fallen short of the glory of God (Romans 3:23).

Rather than coming to the Great Physician with our sickness and our sin, we choose other means. The options are endless, but the result is the same. Our body and soul belong to sin.

In His great love, God created humans endowed with reason and sense. As stewards of creation, we use and develop these gifts.

Medical and scientific advances are great gifts that God provides through us and to us. Nevertheless, we seek alternative means to explain the universe and care for our infirmities. Finding God's Word insufficient, we invite deception as we entertain religious positions foreign to the faith revealed through Jesus Christ.

73. If we know someone to be gifted at healing through alternative means, is it dangerous to use their services? Explain.

74. What does our reason tell us about practices such as aura and crystal healing or psychic surgery?

75. Is it possible to maintain a Christian worldview while pursuing New Age healing techniques? Explain.

The
Treatment

The Pharisees found Jesus sitting amidst sinners, including the former tax collector Matthew. Questioning Jesus' compliance to the Jewish laws and traditions, the Pharisees asked Matthew, "Why does your teacher eat with tax collectors and 'sinners'?" (Matthew 9:11).

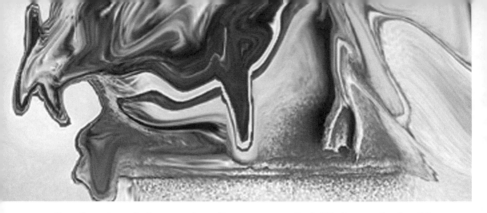

Overhearing their question, Jesus responded, "It is not the healthy who need a doctor, but the sick. But go and learn what this means: 'I desire mercy, not sacrifice.' For I have not come to call the righteous, but sinners" (9:12).

Jesus' words offer comfort and hope for all who share the diagnosis of sin. Despite our previous attempts to find healing elsewhere, Jesus came to provide deeper healing. This is no ordinary health. It is eternal health.

When we experience sickness and ill health, through Christ we can approach God, the Great Physician, for healing. Poor health and sickness appear to run rampant. Cancer and other awful diseases seem to go unchecked. When doctors are unable to cure us and our health fails, the promise of God remains.

The Old Testament figure Job experienced sickness to the point of death. Though his health failed him, Job stood firm in the sure promises of God. "I know that my Redeemer lives, and that in the end He will stand upon the earth. And after my skin has been destroyed, yet in my flesh I will see God" (Job 19:25–26).

We can stand firm with Job in our confession of faith and hope for the future. Christ's death and resurrection assure us of our eternal health and right standing before God.

76. The Pharisees asked Jesus' disciples why He ate with "tax collectors" and "sinners." What do these two character designations say about Jesus' company? What does it say about the nature of Jesus' work on earth and in eternity?

77. Make a list of the names of hospitals in your region or other hospitals you have visited. Based on these names, what conclusions can you reach about the place of healing in the Christian faith? Also read Acts 6:1–6.

78. To whom can we go for sure healing of body and soul? Explain.

Words
to Remember

It is not the healthy who need a doctor, but the sick. But go and learn what this means: "I desire mercy, not sacrifice." For I have not come to call the righteous, but sinners. Matthew 9:12

Leader Notes

Leaders,

The most difficult chapter of this study is chapter one, which introduces the worldview of *monism*. Work through this section patiently. Direct participants to the glossary at the back of the book. Once participants understand how monism differs from Christianity, they will more easily understand the issue of contemporary spirituality.

Please note the different abilities of your class members. Some will easily find Bible passages and pronounce the terms used in this study. Others will struggle. To make participation easier, team up members of the class. For example, if a question asks you to look up several passages, assign one passage to one group, the second to another, and so on. Divide up the work! Let participants present the different answers that they discover. Also, have students turn to the glossary at the back of this book for help with technical terms.

Each topic is divided into four sections.

Focus introduces the topic for discussion.

Science critique summarizes what modern science has discovered about the topic.

Law critique considers the topic in view of God's commands.

Gospel affirmation helps students understand how God addresses the issues raised by the topic through His Son, Jesus Christ.

Enlightened

Objectives: By the power of the Holy Spirit working through God's Word, participants will analyze and demonstrate the uncertainty and danger of contemporary spirituality; encounter God's condemnation of false spirituality; and find assurances of God's promises and the truthfulness of the Christian faith.

1. Answers will vary. Allow for specific examples. Emphasize, however, that you are looking for examples of spiritual belief, not names of people involved. There will be a variety of opinions offered that account for the popularity of this sort of spirituality. Of course, the root of false spirituality is sin, but help the group to see secondary reasons.

Cult researchers and apologists have noted at least two major reasons for this type of spirituality. First, anthropological studies in human history show that when traditional and historic religions decline in a culture, superstitious and individualistic spirituality arises. Walter Martin, founder of the Christian Research Institute, notes that what was once considered New Age spirituality is now considered enlightened spirituality. By assigning scientific names to spiritual practices and drawing connections to scientific research, enlightened New Age spirituality appeals to younger generations. If a spirituality can make scientific claims, it appeals to the noncritical mind.

2. Answers will vary. One of the difficulties with studying spiritual trends such as enlightened spirituality is that people who practice these trends hold views of reality that differ from classic western thought. Even though the trends appear scientific at times, they are grounded in eastern spiritual thought. To understand the logic of a religion or philosophy, you must define how it sees the world (worldview).

3. In his book *The Closing of the American Mind*, Allen Bloom states that by the time a young person enters college, he or she has learned that there is no absolute truth. American culture teaches this pluralism through and through.

The belief that nothing is really true directly challenges Jesus' statement: "I am the way and the truth and the life" (John 14:6). Warning against false teaching, Jude wrote, "I felt I had to write and urge you to contend for the faith that was once for all entrusted to the saints" (Jude 3). In the face of unbelief and false teaching, God calls Christians to proclaim and defend the universal truth of the Gospel. Many attitudes expressed in the *U.S. News and World Report*'s article "Faith in America: It's as important as ever, no matter what you believe" are intellectually sloppy and spiritually destructive. If you hold the truth of the Gospel of Jesus Christ, you must face the claim made by others that nothing is absolutely true.

A Light on the Hidden and Uncertain

4. Groups such as *ShadoWorlds* claim that humans have the power to perceive the invisible aspects of creation. Modern spirituality's thought about creation, visible and invisible, differs from the Christian view. A so-called enlightened spirituality sees no distinction between creation and the Creator. Everything, seen and unseen, is connected by some sort of psychic energy. This energy, if tapped into by an enlightened mind, increases one's awareness of past, present, and future.

Christianity paints a different picture. Christians maintain that God exists apart from creation. That is, God is eternal. Creation depends on God for its existence. Humans depend on God as well.

Reliable knowledge of unseen realities and spiritual truths comes from God. That is, God discloses what He desires humans to know concerning spiritual realities. *ShadoWorlds* and contemporary spirituality work the other way. Humans, by their own psychic abilities, perceive and define their own spirituality.

Arriving at spirituality on our own accord remains uncertain. By its very nature, modern spirituality can never be sure it has drawn the right conclusions from spiritual experiences. However, in Christianity God gives us conclusions that can be trusted because they come from God Himself. Biblical Christian spirituality is the only sure spirituality because the Creator supplies the information.

5. Spiritual experiences do not validate a religion. They could

result from hallucinations, self-deception, or demonic deception. You can never be sure what lies behind spiritual experiences.

There remains only one sure way of validating spirituality. It must come from the author of experience and spirituality Himself. By taking on human flesh, the Author of Life unequivocally demonstrated true spirituality—a spirituality of mercy. Christ's incarnation, death, and resurrection validate this spirituality.

Christianity does not ask a person to try it out and see if your experience validates its truthfulness. Rather, Christianity stands as the truth. The Spirit of God reveals this truth to us. Apart from the Spirit of God, the life, death, and resurrection of Jesus are mere historical facts. The Holy Spirit enlightens our minds in order that we may know that Christ's death was for us. Instructors may want to talk about the work of the Holy Spirit (for help see *The Holy Spirit* by Korey Maas in the Lutheran Difference series by CPH).

The Darkness of Uncertainty

6. Contemporary enlightened spirituality builds off of uncertainty. Mystical experiences, however delightful, do not offer a reliable basis for a spiritual belief system. Like sand, spirituality backed by human experience and opinions does not offer a firm foundation.

Christian spirituality builds on something different. For example, Jesus testified to the authority of the Old and New Testaments. Throughout Jesus' ministry, He quoted the Old Testament Scripture in support of His claims. A key feature of Jesus' ministry was the fulfillment of Old Testament prophecies. Through such testimony and fulfillment, Jesus demonstrated His credibility. Prior to His death, Jesus promised to send the Spirit of truth to His disciples. The Holy Spirit would teach the disciples and remind them of everything Jesus said to them (John 14:26), and He would guide them into all truth (16:13). In this way Jesus shared His authority with the apostles—the writers of the New Testament. God's Word in Christ and in the Scriptures are reliable. From them, Christians receive a firm foundation for faith.

7. Spirituality built without a foundation results in uncertainty and insecurity. Doubt follows uncertainty. "He who doubts is like a wave of the sea, blown and tossed by the wind" (James 1:6). Without

a firm foundation, we cannot stand firmly in God's promises. Foundationless spirituality leads to doubt, despair, and deception.

8. Answers will vary. Allow the class to discuss without fear of condemnation. You may want to find specific examples in advertisements or spiritualistic magazines that use Christian terminology and personalities. For example, many spiritists speak of a cosmic Christ or angelic messengers. Some will even quote Scripture. Because attempts at showing compatibility are often taken out of context, you may want to discuss how Scripture and the person of Christ are distorted in popular spirituality.

Affirm the finality of God's revelation in Christ and the Scriptures. Emphasize that true spirituality can only be informed and shaped by God's revelation. From God's revelation we are informed of the sure means of grace. True spirituality encounters God in His Word and Sacraments. These are the only sure means of spiritual renewal.

9. We are assured of spiritual realities because of God's revelation. Because God is the Creator, He is the only authority on the subject. Check all claims of knowledge about spiritual realities (e.g., angels, human fate) with Scripture. If these claims are not drawn from a proper interpretation of Scripture or contradict Scripture, they must be rejected or corrected.

10. Solomon writes, "The fear of the LORD is the beginning of knowledge" (Proverbs 1:7). All truthful spiritual wisdom and understanding come from God in His Word. We fear the Lord and humbly approach Him by allowing Him to have the final say.

Shedding Light on the Darkness

11. John records that the resurrection assured the disciples of Christ's and the Scripture's authority. "After He was raised from the dead, His disciples recalled what He had said. Then they believed the Scripture and the words that Jesus had spoken" (John 2:22). The resurrection assured the most doubtful that Jesus is "Lord" and "God" (John 20:28). The resurrection of Christ separates the Christian faith from all other religious faiths.

12. After His resurrection, Jesus enlightened His disciples about

the Scriptures. "And beginning with Moses and all the Prophets, He explained to them what was said in all the Scriptures concerning Himself" (Luke 24:27). God incarnate showed His disciples that the Old Testament Scriptures pointed to Christ. In the Old Testament, the story of human redemption unfolded before the time of Christ. Jesus is the key to unlock the Scriptures. Scriptures should be read through the lens of Christ's person and work. That is, the fulfillment of the Law in the Gospel sets the theme of all of Scripture.

13–14. The Holy Spirit works in our hearts and minds through the Scripture and the Sacraments. Repentance results from the working of the Spirit. That is, we are faced with our sin and rebellion against God (contrition), and our minds are changed from trusting ourselves to faith in Christ. The means of grace enlighten our minds to the knowledge of forgiveness of sins and the spirituality shaped by it. God does the work; therefore, it most certainly is true!

CHAPTER TWO

Voice from Beyond

Objectives: By the power of the Holy Spirit working through God's Word, participants will recognize the deception of psychic mediums; observe the connection between psychic consultation and lack of trust in God's Word; and know the certainty of God's revelation in Christ.

15. Answers will vary. Share thoughts while bearing in mind people's reputations. The point is to show that psychic mediums are common and many people seek them out. Often people will go to a psychic because they desperately seek spiritual advice. Many people seek out mediums when faced with questions concerning life after death.

16. Psychics like John Edward see God as an impersonal force. Oftentimes in psychic circles there is no distinction between man and God. Man is typically viewed as either a part of God or a god. God is often referred to as energy. Psychics claim to tap into psychic energy, which allows them to contact others who share in the same psychic divinity.

Many psychic mediums believe in reincarnation or a variation of this teaching. When a person dies, psychics believe the deceased can be contacted. The deceased is typically seen as a bodiless spirit who remains present but is no longer visible. There is no heaven or hell in psychic thought. Man goes on existing eternally as a spirit being who may or may not come back as another person.

Christianity sees death as final. When a person dies, he or she either enters eternal blessedness (heaven) or eternal damnation (hell).

17. Though different opinions may be presented, Christian spirituality cannot be synthesized with psychic spirituality. A psychic worldview not only contradicts Christian teachings on God and humans; it also contradicts the redemption of man won by the death and resurrection of Christ.

Voices
from Beyond?

18. Answers may vary. By our applying knowledge of how hot, warm, and cold readings work, a psychic's spiritual hoax is fairly easy to detect. However, some psychics appear very convincing. The psychic may stumble onto the truth by mere coincidence. Scriptures inform us of other possibilities: the psychic could receive information from the devil or demonic spirits.

19. The terms "passed on" or "crossed over" indicate, though not always, a psychical worldview. Refer to question 16 for a brief analysis of this worldview.

The only certain explanation for our reality is found in the author of our reality. When God created, He brought reality as we know it into existence. A scriptural worldview is informed by the One who created time and space. Scripture offers us a voice from outside the human situation, which informs us of reality.

20. A psychic's god is a false god. The true God who reveals Himself in Scripture commands His people to reject mediums. Hence, a psychic's notion of god cannot be the true God. Following a psychic and his god is idolatry.

When a psychic claims to be gifted by God, he misleads those who trust him. Not only does he lead to false knowledge about God; he leads to a false hope for the future. In the end, he leads to damnation. Trust is placed in man and his false promises rather than the reliable promises of God in Christ.

21. Mediums may not only speak with unidentifiable spirits, as mentioned in number 5 above, but they also offer a false hope in life after death apart from Christ.

Psychics often offer personal advice with tragic consequences. In his book *Psychic Mafia*, former psychic M. Lamar Keene testifies about the dependence of clients on their psychics. As a psychic, he offered all sorts of advice, from marriage to professional, and his clients almost always followed it—many times, he sadly recounts, to their detriment. Marriages dissolved, jobs were lost, and so forth, and still his clients came back. He also tells of how most of the prominent psychics he knew died tragic deaths from alcoholism, mental illness, depression, and the like.

Words
That Condemn

22. Jesus' death and resurrection put to death our old sinful nature and raise us to new life in Christ. They also give a picture of our bodily death. Like Jesus, when we die we will be physically raised from the dead unto eternal life. This bodily resurrection will come at the Last Day when Jesus judges all the living and the dead. Those with faith in Christ will rise to eternal life. Those trusting anyone other than God in Christ will descend to eternal damnation.

23. Samuel responded that the Lord's condemnation on Saul's kingship would remain. Prior to Samuel's death, he delivered these words to Saul: "Does the LORD delight in burnt offerings and sacrifices as much as in obeying the voice of the LORD? To obey is better than sacrifice, and to heed is better than the fat of rams. For rebellion is like the sin of divination, and arrogance like the evil of idolatry. Because you have rejected the word of the LORD, He has rejected you as King" (1 Samuel 15:22–23).

24. Through Samuel, God delivered His word of judgment upon Saul. Yet Saul continued to disobey God. Threatened by the Philistine army, Saul made a final attempt to escape God's judgment. After his prayers went unanswered, Saul sought out a medium. God's original judgment (1 Samuel 15:22–23) compared Saul's rebellion to divination. Faced with imminent judgment, Saul committed the sin of divination itself.

When God speaks, His Word does not change. God's Law does not change. Likewise, His promises do not change. Seeking out mediums treats God's Word as insufficient. The response that the spirit of Samuel gave to Saul demonstrates the sufficiency of God's Word. When God says He will do something, He will prove faithful to His Word. Psychic council undermines God's Word and blatantly doubts God's Word.

25. A common feature of modern spirituality is the mixing of different belief systems (syncretism). For a shocking example, see *The Dummies Guide to Spirituality*.

The One
from the Dead

26. Advice will vary. The message that Jesus' death and resurrection paid the ransom price for sin and defeated death is essential. On the basis of the death and resurrection, God declares man righteous before Him. Death is no longer frightening. The penalty for our sin was paid. God is no longer our judge but rather our redeemer.

27. In the face of unbelief, Christian apologists have used this argument ("myths don't make martyrs") to establish the historicity of the resurrection. The word *martyr* comes from the Greek word that means "to witness or testify." The early Christians were killed because they testified to the resurrection of Jesus Christ. All the apostles, with the exception of John, were killed because of their testimony to Christ's resurrection.

When faced with the choice to either withdraw their claim that Jesus rose from the dead or to die, the apostles chose to die. Why? They *saw* Jesus after His death. To withdraw their testimony was to deny the truth that they saw with their very eyes.

The apostles must have seen Jesus alive after He died. For them to willingly die for a lie they knowingly concocted would have been a miracle in itself. When faced with choosing death for something they claimed to be witnesses to or freedom for denying what they saw, the apostles chose death. Surely myths don't make martyrs.

28. Spiritual beliefs shaped by humans are limited to humans. Humans are bound to their experiences, and our experiences often deceive us. Through Adam, we are born into sin. Because we are sinners, we ignore and rebel against God's promises. In our rebellion, we find ourselves choosing our own path. This path leads to spiritual uncertainty. The only thing for certain is death.

Jesus, born from Adam's seed yet from divine origin, walked the same path that humans walk. He did not rebel against God. Yet He still died. After His death, Jesus returned from the grave. Jesus paved the way to life after death. He made the way from humans to God. Trusting in His work for us, we are led to new life.

29. Answers will vary. According to St. Paul, Christian spirituality is founded in and shaped by Christ. In order to stand firmly in the truth, our spirituality must begin and end in Jesus. Apart from Him, His person and work, our faith is in vain. This is spirituality as God

reveals it. See *The Spirituality of the Cross* by Gene Veith (CPH).

The spirituality of the cross shapes our congregational spirituality as well. Our corporate worship and fellowship focus on Jesus' person and work. The means of grace not only remind us of Christ's death and resurrection; they apply the forgiveness of sins to us. The means of grace certify our forgiveness and right standing before God and one another.

CHAPTER THREE

Your Destiny

Objectives: By the power of the Holy Spirit working through God's Word, participants will detect the spuriousness of astrology; recognize God's condemnation of astrology; and find certainty and assurance in the Gospel.

30. Answers will vary. Horoscopes can be found in every form of media. Newspapers have daily readings. Television and telephone services offer astrological readings. Internet astrologers offer daily readings through e-mail.

Regarding astrology's place in society, answers will vary. Because of its popularity in the media, astrology has a definite place in American society. Horoscopes are a part of many people's lives. People seek out astrologers for personal and professional advice.

31. Answers will vary. The problems associated with astrology will be explored in the following section. However, discuss the class's initial reactions to the question. It is very possible that class participants engage in some form of horoscope reading either for entertainment purposes or for actual advice.

Science and the Stars

32. Answers will vary. Accurate horoscopes could be attributed to a variety of factors. Chance could account for some of the accuracy of astrological readings.

A former astrologer's client (we'll call him Ken) described his last weeks before turning from relying on his astrologer to embracing Christianity. Ken's astrologer told him that he was going to be safe and healthy for at least the next few weeks. A few days later, Ken broke his arm. When Ken asked his astrologer how this could happen in light of his previous astrological reading, the astrologer answered,

"Think of everything else that could have gone wrong. Be happy that you only broke your arm."

33. Every astrologer will claim to offer authentic readings. However, scientific and logical analysis exposes the weaknesses of astrology. There is no evidence supporting claims that celestial bodies dictate human behavior and foretell future events. Though a horoscope or an astrologer may appear accurate, chance and faulty inferences can account for some accuracy.

34. Answers will vary. The author made this observation on the basis of the large number of media appearances by astrologers. Polls and questionnaires show that horoscopes are read and are often considered reliable by people from all religious and cultural backgrounds.

35. Astrologers base their readings on planetary and astral alignments. Hence, an astrologer's authority is the planets and stars. The worldview of astrology connects human behavior and circumstances with the planets and stars. Because celestial bodies dictate human behavior, free will is foreign to the thought of astrologers. With no free will, people have no choice in their behavior or future. The stars dictate human destiny.

There is no room for God in an astrologer's worldview. If everything is ruled by the stars, what place could God have? Though astrologers may speak of God, it is empty talk.

36. Answers will vary. Superstition is rooted in fear and does not seek understanding.

Stars and Scarecrows

37. Both the stars in the sky and wood from a tree are created objects. Both stars and trees owe their existence to the Creator. Without God creating them, the stars and trees would not exist. Worship and trust of created objects bewilders Jeremiah. What would cause someone to trust in a temporal object? Only the living, eternal God, proclaims Jeremiah, deserves worship. He is the only true God (10:10).

Jeremiah compares stars and wood to demonstrate the absurdity of worshiping anything other than the God of Israel. Jeremiah compares fear about "signs in the sky" to an idol carved from a tree. To highlight the foolishness of worshiping man-made idols, Jeremiah compares the impotency of the wooden idol to a scarecrow. "Like a scarecrow in a melon patch, their idols cannot speak; they must be carried because they cannot walk" (10:5). Like a scarecrow, idols carved from trees are powerless. The thought of worshiping them is foolish. Like idols carved from trees, the stars in the sky are powerless. As created objects they have no power over humans.

We could push the argument further to illustrate the logic of reserving worship and reverence for God alone. A scarecrow owes its existence and place in a melon patch to the farmer who puts it there. Therefore, just as a scarecrow owes its existence to the farmer who formed him, we owe our existence to God the Creator. He alone controls and rules our lives. He alone is worthy of worship.

38. To begin with, Israel's neighbors practiced idolatry. Israel was forbidden from practicing idolatry (Second Commandment). The Israelites were to worship the God of Israel alone. Turning away from God's commandments invited God's wrath on Israel. The prophets continually warned against this.

In addition to idol worship, many of Israel's neighbors practiced child sacrifice. Practicing the idolatry of their neighbors could possibly entice Israel from idolatry to more detestable practices. These practices invited God's consuming anger.

39. Answers will vary. In his Large Catechism, Luther explained what it means to fear God. He cites Exodus 20:5–6: "I, the LORD your God, am a jealous God, punishing the children for the sin of the fathers to the third and fourth generation of those who hate Me, but showing love to a thousand generations of those who love Me and keep My commandments." Luther notes that God wants to be feared, not despised. However, Luther notes, God does not let wickedness go unpunished. His anger does not cease until the wicked are exterminated. God's Law judges completely. There is no escape from His punishment. On account of this, we are to fear God. For unlike the mute stars and planets, our Maker speaks His judgment against sin. Our destiny is in His almighty hands.

40. Answers will vary. Trust, fear, and love of God push us to work harder. God blesses us with careers, education, family, and so forth. He entrusts these things to our care. The attitude "I don't need to work hard; God will take care of me" is quite the opposite of what it means to trust God.

We trust God for every good gift. We work hard as stewards of

God's gifts. By fearing God, we strive to keep His commandments. In loving and trusting God, we gladly act according to His commandments.

41. Christian spirituality fears, loves, and trusts in God for all earthly and eternal blessings. Seeking astrological advice violates God's commandments. It finds comfort and hope in created objects. Astrology enthrones created objects as gods and dethrones God, the creator of these very objects.

Christian spirituality places its fear and trust in God alone. God's promise of temporal and eternal blessings assures us of our future. Mature Christian spirituality seeks to fear, love, and trust in God above all things in every part of life.

"Sign" of Salvation

42. Over the centuries, philosophers and theologians have debated issues about free will and predestination. More often than not, these debates end in a stalemate. The Gospel gives us God's answer.

From the beginning, God promised humanity a Savior (Genesis 3:15). God promised this Savior to all. At the appointed time, this promise was fulfilled in Jesus. His saving work effected the forgiveness of sins for all people (1 John 2:2). In Christ, our fate is sealed, our sins forgiven, and our salvation certain. Apart from Christ, we remain accountable for our sin and subject to God's punishment. Reading Scripture through the lens of Christ gives us this answer: salvation is God's work and damnation is man's.

43. The Jewish scholars went right to Scripture. They knew that the only sure information concerning the Messiah had to come from God. The Scriptures record God's Word throughout history.

44. Christianity is designated as *the* world religion. The Magi's visit to Jesus demonstrated this. Some scholars think the Magi may have been Zoroastrians. To be sure, they were not Jews, though they may have had some contact with Jews in their lifetime. In spite of their culture and religion, God led them to their Savior. By using the stars to guide them to Jesus, God met the Magi where they were in their religious understanding. He also fulfilled the prophecy of Numbers 24:15–19.

Contemplate

Objectives: By the power of the Holy Spirit working through God's Word, participants will determine the limits of science in relation to religion; distinguish between artificial and authentic religious experiences; and recognize authentic spirituality and religious experience.

45. Answers will vary. Tell the class that meditation can be understood positively. This theme will be considered below.

46. Answers will vary. Allow the class to discuss issues about science and theology. Avoid bashing science or theology. Science is a gift from God. Science gets in trouble when it speaks outside the realm of its inquiry. Perhaps a discussion on the limits of scientific research would prove fruitful.

47. Meditation can relieve stress involved with work, school, or relationships. Used as a relaxation technique, it can be a great blessing. However, professional meditation facilitators oftentimes have eastern religious influences. Meditation associated with eastern ideas of monism and divine self-awareness contradicts the Christian faith. Christians who practice meditation should be wary of this.

Science and God

48. Neurotheology assumes that observations of human religious experience leads to knowledge of the human relation to God. It assumes that the evidence found within humans gives us data about God.

Analysis of this theological method brings to light a few problems. First, there are no scientific grounds for concluding that evidence found in nature can tell us about the supernatural. Second, the different subjects studied hold to different spiritual beliefs. A person's religious presuppositions affect the way he or she interprets religious experience. For example, some subjects claimed to feel a mystical union with God. Others felt a sense of awareness of a higher reality. Still others talked about an awareness of interconnectedness with all of reality. A Franciscan nun's idea of God is much different from a Buddhist monk's. Which experience proves to be authentic?

A theologian's method of obtaining information about God differs from a neurotheologian's approach. Theologians begin with what God has revealed to man. From there they speak of God within the framework of accepted language and vocabulary. Neurotheologians extract knowledge of God through scientific observation of human brains. There is no way to measure whether these experiences come from God.

49. Answers will vary regarding the strength of Newberg's claim. However, at the very least Newberg's theory and the other natural theological arguments show that it is not irrational or absurd to believe in God. Even so, we remain a long distance from discovering God by scientific means.

Natural proofs for God's existence divide into two approaches. The first are the empirical or evidential approaches. For example, the world exists; therefore, someone or something must have caused it to exist (cosmological). Another example: the apparent design of the universe requires the work of a designer (teleological).

The second kind of approach is rationalistic. For example, all people have a sense of moral law or right and wrong; therefore, a moral lawgiver (God) must have placed this knowledge in humankind (moral argument). Another example: a higher power must exist because it is absurd to think that there is no higher power among the powers in the universe (ontological argument).

50. As noted above, natural theology at the very least shows that it is not absurd to believe in God. Scientists, philosophers, and theologians have developed extensive proofs that they claim make it absurd to not believe in God. However, these proofs from time to time meet challenges. The church reformer John Calvin claimed that natural theology is at its best when it renders man without an excuse for disbelief.

Natural theology is limited to knowledge of God. The Gospel cannot be found in natural theology. Though theologies drawn from nature offer some insight into the nature of God as Creator and Judge, the Gospel is only found in revealed theology—theology drawn from Christ and the Scriptures.

Different Gospels
Be Damned

51. God told Moses that He would come to him in a dense cloud. The Israelites would hear God speaking to Moses. God did this so that the Israelites would know to trust Moses and the words he delivered from God.

This experience must have been awesome in the true sense of the word. Moses did not talk about subjective and private feelings of interconnectedness. This was a public display of God's glorious presence.

52. God began His dialogue with Moses by identifying Himself as the One who delivered the Israelites from the Egyptians. Immediately God made a promise: "Out of all nations you will be My treasured possession. Although the whole earth is Mine, you will be for Me a kingdom of priests and a holy nation" (Exodus 19:5–6). God's promise was connected with a covenant. Shortly thereafter, God gave the Ten Commandments to the Israelites. They were to obey them, and as a result God would bless them as a nation.

God's covenant showed that He desired to be in relationship with His people. The chapters that follow in Exodus lay out how God's people were to approach Him. These regulations would identify the Israelites as God's chosen and blessed people. This relationship was not based on religious feelings, but a specific set of rules and promises given by God.

53. Knowing that Satan is the great deceiver, we should remain cautious of religious experiential claims that contradict the Gospel. Claims of religious experience could be explained by Newberg's research. That is, neurological processes in the brain cause certain feelings that people interpret as religious experiences.

54. Christian worship should always line up with the Scriptures, the Law and the Gospel. Our worship should always present the biblical message of the Gospel. God established means by which we can be certain our worship is biblical. When the Gospel is preached and the Sacraments are distributed rightly, we can be sure that our worship is genuinely Christian and, hence, our worship experiences are authentically Christian.

Free to Experience the Gospel

55. Answers will vary. Remind the class that the Holy Spirit works through the Law to bring about contrition and through the Gospel to work faith in our hearts and minds.

56. The promises of God in Christ offer comfort for anxiety and fear. Notice the psalmist's words: "I put my hope in Your word." The Scriptures give us authentic and reliable words from God.

57. Authentic religious experience begins and ends with Jesus. God meets man in the person and work of Christ. God in Christ treated our sin and inability to experience God's mercy in His death. He took upon Himself our sin and suffered our punishment on the cross. Jesus' resurrection from the grave guarantees His victory over sin and death. Now we are able to approach God with confidence.

CHAPTER FIVE

Magickal Mystery

Objectives: By the power of the Holy Spirit working through God's Word, participants will recognize the dangers involved with witchcraft and magick; view witchcraft as a spiritual threat; and find comfort and assurance in the power of the Gospel.

58. Answers will vary. You may want to do some research in order to show the presence of Wiccanism and its variations in your area.

59. Answers will vary. Though some who practice witchcraft may not be involved with the occult at first, the danger exists for future involvement.

Recognizing Wiccanism is difficult. Many modern witches are "normal" people. For example, Detective Constable Charles Ennis served on the Vancouver Police Department for years before identifying himself as a Wiccan priest. He continues to serve as an officer, specializing in the investigation of "unusual" crimes.

Magick, Drugs, Sex, and Psychosis

60. Psychiatrists attribute psychological problems in witches to drug use and constant self-deception. The more a witch believes in her powers, the more her perceptions of reality decrease.

Some psychiatrists ascribe psychological problems in witches to demonic possession. Witchcraft has definite ties to the occult. Psychiatrists see a definite connection between occult practices and demonic possession. Since medieval times, witches have been associated with the broad diagnosis of "hysteria." The stereotype of a witch as a lonely, hostile older woman may have its root in cases of mental illness and the isolation that such women experienced.

61. Apart from the psychological and spiritual dangers, involve-

ment with Wiccanism opens one up to physical danger. Magick rites vary from coven to coven. Some are physically harmless. Black magick involves sacrificial rites. Though human sacrifice is rare, scarification and other physical dangers are a real threat.

A Spiritual Showdown

62. Paul accuses Elymas of being a child of the devil. He identifies him as deceitful. His sorcery was used to distract the proconsul from hearing the Word of God. Paul identifies this distraction as a perversion of the right ways of the Lord.

63. Paul blinds Elymas. He shows that the apostolic authority given by Christ overcomes the power of sorcery. Through this miraculous sign, God establishes Paul's authority as a messenger of His Word.

64. The elements of the Old Testament civil code do not apply today. Rather than attack witches, Christians should witness to them as they would to people of other religions. Note that Paul never called for Elymas's execution.

Eternal Certainty

65. Ezekiel prophesied that Baptism would give people a new heart and the indwelling of God's Holy Spirit. Paul compared Baptism to a new circumcision. He spoke of Baptism connecting a person to Christ's death and resurrection, by which Christ defeated the spiritual forces of this world.

66. Christ promised His disciples the authority to free people from their sins. He fulfilled this after His resurrection when He called the apostles to proclaim the forgiveness of sins.

67. Answers will vary. Using the Law to demonstrate the false assumptions that Wiccanism holds as well as the false gods it worships, Christians can throw light on the uncertainty and danger that Wiccans engage in. The Gospel brings certainty and safety to those in darkness and uncertainty.

CHAPTER SIX

Body and Mind

Objectives: By the power of the Holy Spirit working through God's Word, participants will see the underlying assumptions and scientific spuriousness of many alternative healing and health practices, recognize the spiritual dangers involved in alternative healing and health; and stand firm in the promise of eternal health for both body and soul through Christ.

68. Answers will vary. The exercises taught by yoga may contribute to a healthy lifestyle. Though many yoga adherents claim spiritual benefits as well, Christians can practice yoga without fear so long as they reject the spiritual teaching of many yoga teachers.

New Age healers can be dangerous. Relying on unscientific methods for healing requires a great leap of faith. Waiting for results from a psychic healer could lead to more health problems.

Health and Science

69. Yes. Christians may use the exercises associated with yoga, but need to be wary of the spiritual claims of eastern philosophies that often accompany yoga.

70. Answers will vary. Alternative medicines offer miracle cures. Just as some Christian groups flock to faith healers, New Agers seek out healers for the same reasons.

When a person is engaged in New Age and eastern thought, he or she may lose trust in western medicines. An eastern worldview caters to alternative healers and physical-spiritual exercises.

71. Answers will vary. Some alternative medicines have some scientific support. For example, acupuncture can offer relief from pain where other treatments have failed. However, science has been able to verify a cause/effect relationship between acupuncture and pain

responses in the brains of animal and human patients. Most alternative treatments lack such verification. Use careful scrutiny when considering alternative health options.

72. Answers will vary. To begin with, these practices may lead a person into false religious practices. Moreover, these practices have no scientific basis. Because they are connected with the occult, they pose serious spiritual dangers. While waiting for healing using alternative means, a person could grow sicker by not seeking adequate, qualified medical attention.

The Diagnosis

73. Answers will vary. See the answers given above.

74. Our reason casts serious doubts on these practices. Science does not support them. The religious assumptions of these healers contradict a Christian worldview. There really is no reason to trust these types of healers.

75. No. By seeking out New Age healers, you are condoning and trusting in their religious assumptions.

The Treatment

76. Jesus kept company with society's worst sinners. Tax collectors were at the lowest rung of the social ladder. Selling out to the Roman government, tax collectors often cheated their own people out of money. For this they were considered to be equivalent with prostitutes and other "gross" sinners.

Jesus' words ring true. He did not spend all His time with the religious elite. Rather, He associated with the outcasts, the sick, and the unclean. Jesus' work on the cross brings eternal healing and salvation to all regardless of social and religious status.

77. Most hospitals have an association with Christianity. Modern medical care has its roots in the institutional care that Christians provided for the sick as early as the fourth century (*nosokomeia*). As the

Book of Acts shows, Christians followed Christ's example by caring for the body as well as the soul.

78. Jesus is the only sure source of healing. Though doctors and exercise are great blessings, apart from Jesus we have no certainty of body and soul.

Glossary

aura An energy field, which some believe emanates from a living being.

contrition To feel sorry for one's sin.

enlightened Full of spiritual insight.

Gospel The message of Christ's death and resurrection for the forgiveness of sins. The Holy Spirit works through the Gospel to create faith and convert people.

Law God's will, which shows people how they should live (e.g., the Ten Commandments) and condemns their failure. The preaching of the Law is the cause of contrition.

medium A person who claims the ability to communicate with the dead.

monism The belief that everything that exists has one substance or ultimate reality (e.g., no distinction between mind and matter).

phenomenon An object or event known through the senses.

Santeria Occult beliefs and rituals in which Roman Catholic saints represent gods from Yoruba, a West African religion. Santeria originated in Cuba and involves ritual sacrifice.

spirituality Personal religious interest or sensitivity; recognizing that more than the material world exists.

paranormal Events or experiences that surpass normal sensory experience, such as ESP, telekinesis, and psychic ability.

psychic A person sensitive to nonphysical forces such as thoughts, feelings, or spirits.

worldview How one looks at the universe and his or her place in it, so that one can make moral decisions.